Our Planet Earth

VOLCANOES

Please visit our web site at: **www.garethstevens.com**
**For a free color catalog describing Gareth Stevens Publishing's list of
high-quality books and multimedia programs, call 1-800-542-2595 (USA)
or 1-800-387-3178 (Canada). Gareth Stevens Publishing's fax: (414) 332-3567.**

Library of Congress Cataloging-in-Publication Data available upon request from
publisher. Fax (414) 336-0157 for the attention of the Publishing Records Department.

ISBN 0-8368-3385-6

This edition first published in 2004 by
Gareth Stevens Publishing
A World Almanac Education Group Company
330 West Olive Street, Suite 100
Milwaukee, WI 53212 USA

This U.S. edition copyright © 2004 by Gareth Stevens, Inc. First published in
1999 as *Blast: The Volcano Files* by Discovery Enterprises, LLC, Bethesda,
Maryland. © 1999 by Discovery Communications, Inc.

Further resources for students and educators available at
www.discoveryschool.com

Designed by Bill SMITH STUDIO
Creative Director: Ron Leighton
Designers: Eric Hoffsten, Jay Jaffe, Brian Kobberger, Nick Stone,
    Sonia Gauba
Production Directors: Peter Lindstrom, Paula Radding
Photo Editor: Justine Price
Art Buyer: Lillie Caporlingua

Gareth Stevens Editor: Betsy Rasmussen
Gareth Stevens Art Director: Tammy Gruenewald
Technical Advisor: Emily Watson

Printed in the United States of America

1 2 3 4 5 6 7 8 9 08 07 06 05 04

Writer: Jacqueline A. Ball

Editors: Marc Gave, Lynn Brunelle, David Krasnow.

Photographs: Cover, © Discovery Communications, Inc.;
p. 3, upper right, and p. 9, second from top, Folsom, Lucius
G./NGS Image Collection; p. 8-9, all except second from top
p. 9, United States Geophysical Survey (U.S.G.S.); p. 11,
Erich Lessing/Art Resource, NY Inc.; p. 13, Mary Shelley,
© Discovery Communications, Inc.; Frankenstein, The Image
Bank; p. 14, top, U.S.G.S.; p. 15, © Discovery Communications,

Inc.; p. 22, © Ragnar Larusson/Science Source/Photo
Researchers, Inc.; p. 26, Mark Twain, The Image Bank,
© Discovery/Archive Photos; Kilauea, U.S.G.S.; p. 28, Maurice
and Katia Krafft, Krafft/Explorer/Science Source/Photo
Researchers, Inc.; Steve and Donna O'Meara, © 1999 by
Steve and Donna O'Meara, Volcano Watch International;
p. 29, © Discovery/Tony Stone Images.

Illustration: pp. 4-5, Patricia J. Wynne and Dianne Gaspas;
pp. 18-19, Joe LeMonnier; pp. 20-21, Patricia J. Wynne and
Dianne Gaspas.

Discovery
CHANNEL
SCHOOL
SCIENCE

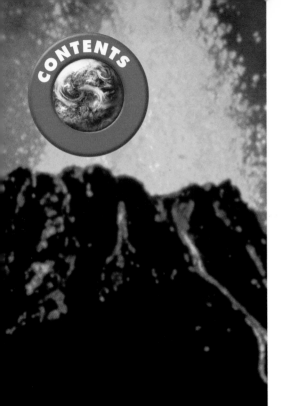

VOLCANOES

Volcanoes. In Roman mythology, they were caused by Vulcan, god of fire, which is how they got their name. Vulcan worked at a forge underground, hammering out metal weapons for the other gods. Explosions were the sparks from his hammer. In Hawaiian legends, a lava-haired goddess named Pele was responsible. Today, volcanologists use scientific methods and tools to learn more about what goes on inside Earth to cause these astounding phenomena.

In VOLCANOES, Discovery Channel takes you from inside Earth to the stratosphere to show you what power volcanoes have to shape history and change lives. Maybe even your own.

For my next act . . . see page 9.

3

Volcano

Ever try to hold back a sneeze . . . or a burp? You feel the pressure building up, and you just can't stop it. It's not your fault. It's nature's way.

An active volcano is like a giant sneeze. Melted rock (magma) mixed with gases is forced up from miles underground. As pressure builds, it erupts through the thin crust that separates Earth's inside from its outside. Like a runny nose, a small opening may ooze a trickle of hot melted rock. Just as some sneezes are polite little a-choos, sometimes this molten rock relieves its pressure gradually, in small pops. And just as some sneezes are tissue-shredders, sometimes the hot stuff blasts its way out with a force that takes off the top of the mountain. See for yourself what's inside a volcano and what comes out. Refer back to this page as often as you want while you read the book.

ERUPTION CLOUD—Cloud coming from a volcano that contains tephra (ash) and gas.

CONE—Mountain in a cone shape that is built up layer by layer through many eruptions.

LAVA—Magma that has erupted from a volcano.

VOLCANO STATUS:

DORMANT—Has erupted in the past and may erupt again, but is not now erupting.

ACTIVE—Currently erupting or dormant.

EXTINCT—Has not erupted for a very long period of time.

PYROCLASTICS—Rock fragments blasted out of an exploding volcano. They can form fast-moving flows full of hot gas that are much more quickly destructive than molten lava flows.

POISONOUS GASES:
Carbon dioxide (CO_2)
Hydrogen fluoride (HF)
Hydrogen sulfide (H_2S)
Sulfur dioxide (SO_2)
Hydrogen chloride (HCl)

CRATER—Top of central vent that has widened over a number of eruptions.

CENTRAL VENT—Hole at the top of a volcano through which magma erupts.

SIDE VENT—Another hole, or crack, in Earth's surface that connects with the feeder tube and through which magma can also erupt.

FEEDER TUBE—Long passage in Earth that transports magma to the surface.

Layers of Earth

CRUST—Topmost layer of Earth.

MANTLE—Begins 3 to 25 miles (5 to 40 kilometers) beneath Earth's surface.

MAGMA—Hot liquid rock and gases in Earth's mantle or crust. The magma chamber is a pool that feeds a volcano.

CORE—Begins 1,800 miles (2,896 km) beneath Earth's surface and extends to the center.

MAGMA THE MAGNIFICENT TELLS ALL!

Q: You're magma. What's it like to be so hot?

A: Pretty cool, except for all the pressure. I'm sitting under miles of crust, and it weighs billions of tons. Unbelievable. Sometimes I just can't take it. That's why it's nice to escape to the surface through a volcano. The instant I hit the surface, I turn into lava and flow. Magma, lava, lava, magma—we're the same hot stuff: melted rock with a bunch of gases mixed in.

Q: That's cool.

A: No, hot. Molten. Red-hot. We are talking two thousand degrees Fahrenheit, or eleven hundred degrees Celsius. Hot, hot, hot. Many times as hot as boiling water.

Q: OK, OK, you're hot. So do you only hang around in volcanoes, or are you anywhere else underground?

A: ANYWHERE else? You've got to be kidding. Magma is EVERYWHERE else underground! Except for one thin solid part on top, Earth's mantle is all me, myself, and I. You're sitting on magma right now. But don't get up. I'm at least 20 miles or 32 kilometers down.

Q: Wait a minute. If you're everywhere underground, why aren't volcanoes everywhere up here?

A: Well, there ARE five hundred active volcanoes in the world. About sixty of them blow up every year. So I do my best. Seriously, volcanoes don't just happen anywhere. I need the right place in Earth's crust before I can surface.

Q: And the right place is . . . ?

A: It's where the crust is so thin it's cracked, or it's got a hole in it. That's when I make my move. Either I blast out or spill out, depending on my type.

Q: What do you mean, your type? Isn't magma all the same?

A: No way. I come in four different types: andesite, basalt, dacite, and rhyolite. It's like having four different personalities. My basalt type is thin. It's weak. It's got no guts. I have to accept that. It makes bubbles and sprays and pretty fountains of lava and stuff when it erupts. My other kinds are thicker. They're strong. They're powerful. They rule! They make the best blasts, especially rhyolite, which is the thickest of all.

Q: You mean the type of explosion depends on the type of magma?

A: You got it.

Q: But why should it matter whether magma is thin or thick?

A: Come on, figure it out! Think of sipping water through a straw. Slides right up, doesn't it? Now imagine slurping up a mouthful of ketchup through the same straw. See how it works? It's harder for the thicker stuff to rise. And you know what that means.

Q: No, what?

A: It means trouble, and you spell that G-A-S. See, as I rise to Earth's surface, gases down here in the mantle rise too. Because of the pressure, those gases are trying to mix into Magma the Magnificent. When I'm thin and basaltic, that's no problem. I let them right in. We mix up, easy as pie. They dissolve, and we all float up the old vent and spray out the top. Then they drift quietly into the air, maybe making a little plop or whoosh or something. It's like popping the top of your can of cola VERY carefully, a little bit at a time. But when I'm thick—whole different story.

Q: What happens when you're thick?

A: I get stubborn. I block up the magma chamber like a big toe caught in your bathtub drain. The gases all crowd together below and around me. They want to get through, and I won't give. Ha! They bunch up in pockets and sit there fuming and expanding until finally—BLAMMO! This time it's like you shake and shake your cola and then rip off the top and spray it all over the place! We all blast out of there quicker than you can say "stratovolcano!"

Q: Strato-huh?

A: Stratovolcano. That's the kind of volcano made by the biggest blasts and the thicker kinds of magma. Mount St. Helens is a stratovolcano. So is Mount Vesuvius in Italy, and Mount Pelee in Martinique, and tons of other big guys. They're tall and steep, with sides all built up by lava and rock. Another name for them is composite.

Q: If thicker magma makes stratovolcanoes, what do volcanoes made by basaltic magma—the thinner kind—look like?

A: Kind of round and wide. Sort of like what a giant shield would look like if you laid it flat on the ground. That's why they're called shield volcanoes. Hawaii is full of them. In fact, the Hawaiian Islands **are** shield volcanoes.

Q: So you can tell just by looking at a volcano what kind of magma was inside? And what kind of explosion made it? Cool!

A: No, hot, I keep telling you. But you're right. And there's one other way to tell.

Q: What's that?

A: Find a volcano. Wait for it to blow up. See what comes out! Speaking of which—I gotta cool off. I'm outta here.

Activity

POUR IT ON The thickness of a liquid such as magma is called its viscosity, or resistance to flow. The viscosity of magma depends on its temperature, water content, and the amount of a mineral called silica in it. The thicker the magma, the more silica in it.

To get an idea of how viscosity works for common liquids, try this experiment: Take a board about 3 feet (1 meter) long. Tilt the board at a 45-degree angle so that its bottom rests in a sink or on a table with a washable covering. Now, take common liquids of different thicknesses—water, liquid soap, rubbing alcohol, corn syrup, molasses, ketchup, and so forth—and pour a small amount of each into a liquid measuring cup, one at a time.

Pour each liquid onto the top of the board. Time its flow until it reaches the sink. How long does each one take to get to the bottom of the board? Try varying the angle of the board and the temperature of the liquids. What happens?

Just Say "A'a"

Flaming fountains of lava shooting out of a volcano are thrilling and beautiful. But those fireworks usually fade fast. Lava begins to cool right away. What it looks like as it cools depends on a few things: the minerals and elements that make it up, the amount of gas in it, and the lava's viscosity. Check out the following lava lingo and lineup.

LIQUID FIRE

A'a (AH-ah)—Hawaiian term for viscous lava that cools quickly and hardens into a rough, spiky surface

Pahoehoe (pa HOY hoy)—Hawaiian term for thin lava that cools more slowly and hardens into smooth, ropy coils

Kilauea, Hawaii, June 3, 1866

"Jets of lava sprung hundreds of feet into the air and burst into rocket-sprays that returned to the earth in a crimson rain . . ."
—*Mark Twain and the Volcano*

BOMBS AWAY

Bombs—Big chunks of half-molten, half-solid lava

Blocks—Another name for bombs

Blocks and bombs are named according to shape:
Ribbon   Spindle
Cow-dung   Bread crust (shown at left)

SOLID AS A ROCK

Pyroclastics—Hardened lava and solid particles blasted out of a volcano. Here are some kinds of pyroclastics:

Lapilli—Little hardened stones of lava

Pumice (PUM iss)— Lightweight rock full of air pockets

What happens, exactly, when a mountain blasts out tons of these materials all at once? Go back two thousand years and see for yourself on the next page.

Pele's hair—Glass strands formed by water blowing through liquid lava (named for Pele, the Hawaiian volcano goddess)

Ash—Small pyroclastic fragments

Activity

MODEL BEHAVIOR

Make your own clay models of lava and pyroclastic fragments. You can use the baking or nonbaking type of clay, depending on available facilities, time, and whether you want permanent models. For different types of lava flows, look at some pictures that show the characteristic shapes of a'a and pahoehoe. Follow the picture in making your model, or use your imagination to construct a volcanic landscape of your own design.

Use the following size chart as a guide for pyroclastic fragments:

Bomb	More than 2.5 inches (6.4 centimeters) across; can be as large as a house
Lapilli	0.1 to 2.5 inches (.25 cm to 6.4 cm)
Ash	Less than 0.1 inch (.25 cm)
Dust	Powdery

THE BLACKEST DAY

Vesuvius, Italy, A.D. 79

Mount Vesuvius

Pompeii

Misenum

Herculaneum

Plain of Sarno

ITALY

MOUNT VESUVIUS ERUPTS

PLINY THE YOUNGER LIVES TO TELL ABOUT IT!

PLINY THE YOUNGER

For two days beginning August 24, the city of Pompeii (pom-PAY), Italy, was buried under tons of stone and ash as Mount Vesuvius erupted. The eruption claimed the lives of three thousand people, including an admiral and statesman named Pliny (PLINN-ee) the Elder. His nephew, seventeen-year-old Pliny the Younger, watched the disaster from the nearby town of Misenum and then fled. He wrote down details in two letters he sent to his friend Tacitus, a historian. The letters have survived, and they form the oldest recorded eyewitness account of a volcanic eruption. These are excerpts from those letters.

My uncle was at that time with the fleet under his command at Misenum. About one in the afternoon, my mother desired him to observe a cloud of very unusual size and appearance. I cannot give you a more exact description of its figure than by comparing it to a pine tree, for it shot up at a great height in the form of a trunk, which extended itself at the top into several branches.

My uncle ordered large galleys to be launched, and he went aboard one with the intention of assisting many others, where villas stand extremely thick upon the coast. Cinders, which grew thicker and hotter, fell into the ships, followed by pumice stones blackened, scorched, and cracked by fire. The sea ebbed suddenly from under them, while the shore was blocked up with landslides from the mountains.

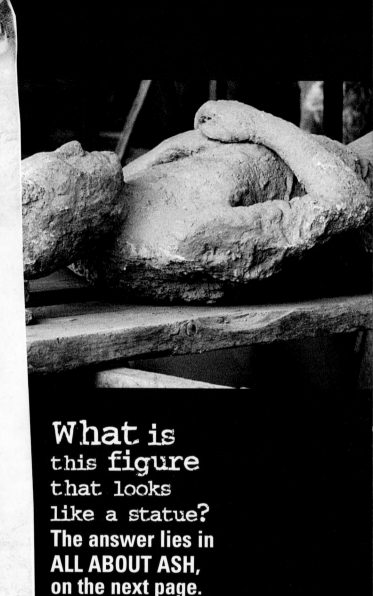

What is this figure that looks like a statue?
The answer lies in **ALL ABOUT ASH,** on the next page.

My uncle having set out, I gave the rest of the day to study, after which I bathed, dined, and retired for short and broken slumbers. It was now six o'clock in the morning. The buildings around us already tottered, and we resolved to quit the town. Outside we halted in the midst of a most strange and dreadful scene. We beheld the sea sucked back, and as if it were repulsed by the convulsive motions of the earth; it is certain at least the shore was considerably enlarged, and now held many sea animals captive on the dry sand. On the other side, a black and dreadful cloud bursting out in gusts of igneous serpentine vapor now and again yawned open to reveal long fantastic flames, resembling flashes of lightning but much larger.

Soon afterwards, the cloud I have described began to descend upon the earth and cover the sea. Taking my mother by the hand, I hurried her on. Ashes now fell upon us. I looked behind me; gross darkness pressed upon our rear and came rolling over the land after us like a torrent. I proposed to turn aside while we yet could see, lest we be knocked down in the road by a crowd that followed us, and trampled to death in the dark. You could hear the shrieks of women and crying children, and the shouts of men. Many were lifting their hands to the gods, but the greater part were imagining that there were no gods left anywhere, and that the last and eternal night had come upon the world.

Activity

WRITING RIGHT Both scientists and writers need to be good observers. Look back carefully at the details and list all the elements Pliny includes, both factual and descriptive, to make this a powerful account.

All About Ash

Herculaneum, Italy, August 24, A.D. 79

When Mount Vesuvius blew its lid on August 24, it released an incredible amount of ash, pumice, and gas. With the addition of rain, the ash and pumice became like wet cement that hardened around the people of Pompeii. Their soft body parts decayed, and the ash and pumice became solid rock. The shapes of the bodies were preserved as hollows in the rock.

The ash cloud that spread over Pompeii missed Herculaneum, a coastal resort town. But something worse was waiting for people there. The town was blasted by a number of pyroclastic surges—avalanches of burning ash and gases that race down a volcano's slope at hurricane speeds. Eventually Herculaneum was buried under 65 feet (20 m) of debris—four or five times as much as what covered Pompeii.

Volcanic ash can cause tremendous harm to everything near it. But you may be surprised to find out that ash can have effects far, far away—effects that can last forever.

ITALY

Passy, France, 1784

During several of the summer months of the year 1783, when the effect of the sun's rays to heat the earth in these northern regions should have been greater, there existed a constant fog over all Europe, and great part of North America. This fog was of a permanent nature; it was dry, and the rays of the sun seemed to have little effect towards dissipating it, as they easily do a moist fog, arising from water. They were indeed rendered so faint in passing through it, that when collected in the focus of a burning glass, they would scarce kindle brown paper.

The cause of this universal fog is not yet ascertained. Whether it was adventitious to [came from] this earth . . . or whether it was the vast quantity of smoke, long continuing; to issue during the summer . . . from Iceland, which smoke might be spread by various winds, over the northern part of the world, is yet uncertain.

The idea that a smoky cloud could block the Sun's heat and cause cold and foggy weather was suggested by Benjamin Franklin. Scientists say he was probably referring to a volcano in Iceland named Laki.

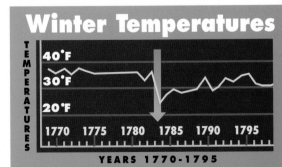

Winter Temperatures

TEMPERATURES

40°F
30°F
20°F

1770 1775 1780 1785 1790 1795

YEARS 1770-1795

After Laki erupted in 1783, look what happened to temperatures in the eastern United States!
(40° F=4.4° C; 30° F=-1.1° C; 20° F=-6.7° C)

Mary Wollstonecraft Shelley was nineteen years old and vacationing with her husband on the shore of Lake Geneva. The summer weather, which had been beautiful, suddenly changed to fierce rains and unbelievable lightning storms. On the night of June 16, the weather made it impossible for the Shelleys to return to their lodgings, so they spent the night with the poet Lord Byron at the villa he was renting. After reading aloud from a collection of ghost stories, Byron challenged his guests to write their own stories.

The others got tired of the challenge, but Mary kept writing. She was further inspired by a discussion several evenings later about whether a scientist could produce life in a humanoid built from human parts. That night she had "a waking nightmare" and arrived at the basis of *Frankenstein*, the novel that gave rise to the modern monster story.

We owe the creation of this story to a volcano! Perhaps as strange as *Frankenstein* itself, the bad weather was most likely caused by fine volcanic dust that had drifted over Earth from the gigantic eruption of Mount Tambora in Indonesia. By the time the dust had been blowing for a year, the world's climate had changed significantly. It was known as the Year Without a Summer, and in the northeastern United States, 1816 was so cold people packed up and headed west.

Lewiston, Maine, June 1816

Dear Diary:
It's so cold! Folks are calling this year "eighteen hundred and froze to death." It snowed last night, and this afternoon Mama's wash froze on the clothesline. Papa says we're moving to Ohio. He says it's warmer there, and we can start a new farm. This one is ruined. All the crops died in the cold and we had to kill the cattle because there was nothing to feed it. Seems that everyone in these parts is packing up and leaving. Pray it's warmer in Ohio.

Activity

BITS AND PIECES

Start collecting interesting tidbits about volcanoes in your own scrapbook. Look for magazine and newspaper articles, pictures, memorabilia. Have it reflect your own personality. It can be organized into categories or chronologically or not organized at all. Include your own artwork if you like. Let your imagination erupt!

THE MYSTERY OF THE
FATAL FUMES

A Remote Island in the North Atlantic, Anytime

Something is very, very wrong. Worldwide, temperatures have dropped by 1 degree Fahrenheit — about .56 degrees Celsius. Doesn't sound like much? One degree can shorten growing seasons, ruining crops all over the world. It's a big problem, and your fellow scientists trace the source of it to a remote agricultural island in the North Atlantic. **You are asked to go investigate.**

It's raining when you arrive. There are no boats in the harbor. A strong wind blows from the west. Judging from the way the trees have grown, this is the way the wind usually blows. Immediately you notice a faint rotten-egg odor. You head against the wind, looking for clues:

▶ Using your high-powered telescope, you look at a still-smoking, gently sloped volcano on the outskirts of a small town. Smooth, ropy coils of lava have covered acres and acres of land around it.

▶ As you adjust your telescope, you see a bird fly over the crater—and drop like a stone.

▶ Leaving the harbor, you walk several miles west of the volcano and find the center of town. Buildings are undamaged. There are no signs of fire. But the town is completely deserted.

▶ You enter the general store. The shelves have been stripped of supplies. On the floor is a page of a calendar turned to February —eight months earlier.

▶ You leave town and walk west, looking for more clues. You pass only deserted farmland. The crops look dead.

▶ Finally, miles away, you come upon a small farmhouse. The remains of a cow are lying in a field. You move the body a little and see that the grass

underneath is covered with a fine white dust.

▶ Cornstalks stand withered and blackened in a row. A bucket is overturned next to them. At the edge of the cornfield is a small farm pond. The smell of rotten eggs is stronger.

▶ You dread going into the farmhouse. What will you find? But eventually, you do—and are relieved to find two elderly people alive. They're surrounded by empty water bottles and food containers. They're very thin and so weak they can hardly talk—and you can't understand their language. The mystery is yours alone to solve.

Answer is on page 32.

Use these clues to help you figure out what may have killed this cow—and to solve the rest of the mystery as well.

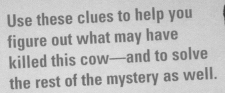

SOME COMMON VOLCANIC GASES

CARBON DIOXIDE (CO_2)—Odorless gas humans breathe out. In high concentration, as suffocating as putting a pillow over your face.

HYDROGEN SULFIDE (H_2S)—Gas with the foul smell of rotten eggs. It can mix with water vapor to form sulfuric acid, then fall as acid rain to pollute lakes and streams and kill plant life and fish. In big or long-lasting volcanic eruptions, sulfuric acid can form a haze that gets into the upper atmosphere, bouncing the Sun's rays away from Earth and causing worldwide cooling.

HYDROGEN FLUORIDE (HF)—Forms a deadly concentrated dust that collects on plants and is fatal to animals. (Don't worry. Fluoride in your toothpaste is too small a dose to harm you.)

SULFUR DIOXIDE (SO_2)—Produces poisonous, corrosive fumes.

This mystery is based on specifics from a real eruption at Laki, Iceland, in 1783, which deposited more than 3.3 cubic miles (14 cubic km) of basaltic lava. Scientists think Laki lowered worldwide temperatures by 1° F (.56° C).

Big Bad Blasts

Deadliest Eruptions

Deaths	Volcano	When	Major Cause of Death
92,000	**Tambora**, Indonesia	1815	**Starvation**
36,417	**Krakatau**, Indonesia	1883	**Tsunami**
29,025	**Mt. Pelée**, Martinique	1902	**Ash flows**
23,000+	**Ruiz**, Colombia	1985	**Mud flows**
14,300	**Unzen**, Japan	1792	**Volcano collapse, tsunami**
9,350	**Laki**, Iceland	1783	**Starvation**
5,110	**Kelut**, Indonesia	1919	**Mud flows**
4,011	**Galunggung**, Indonesia	1822	**Mud flows**
3,500	**Vesuvius**, Italy	1631	**Mud flows, lava flows**
3,360	**Vesuvius**, Italy	79	**Ash flows and falls**
2,957	**Papandayan**, Indonesia	1772	**Ash flows**
2,942	**Lamington**, Papua N.G.	1951	**Ash flows**
2,000	**El Chicon**, Mexico	1982	**Ash flows**
1,680	**Soufriere**, St. Vincent	1902	**Ash flows**
1,475	**Oshima**, Japan	1741	**Tsunami**
1,377	**Asama**, Japan	1783	**Ash flows, mud flows**
1,335	**Taal**, Philippines	1911	**Ash flows**
1,200	**Mayon**, Philippines	1814	**Mud flows**
1,184	**Agung**, Indonesia	1963	**Ash flows**
1,000	**Cotopaxi**, Ecuador	1877	**Mud flows**
800	**Pinatubo**, Philippines	1991	**Roof collapses and disease**
700	**Komagatake**, Japan	1640	**Tsunami**
700	**Ruiz**, Colombia	1845	**Mud flows**
500	**Hibok-Hibok**, Philippines	1951	**Ash flows**

Volcano Trivia

Tallest active volcano
(measuring below sea level):
▶ **Mauna Loa,**
Hawaii 30,000 feet (9,144 m) from the ocean floor

Tallest active volcano
(measuring at sea level):
▶ **Ojos del Salado,**
in Chile, measuring 22,589 feet (6,885 m) tall

Most eruptions in the twentieth century:
▶ **Furnace Peak,**
in the Indian Ocean (80 times since 1900)

Longest continuous eruption in the twentieth century:
▶ **Kilauea,**
Hawaii (20 years as of publication)

How Big Are Eruptions?

The VEI (Volcanic Explosivity Index) indicates how powerful an eruption is. Every year about sixty volcanoes erupt, but most of the activity is fairly weak.

VEI	Description	Plume Height	Classification	How Often	Example
0	non-explosive	<100 m	Hawaiian	daily	Kilauea
1	gentle	100-1000 m	Haw/Strombolian	daily	Stromboli
2	explosive	1-5 km	Strom/Vulcanian	weekly	Galeras, 1992
3	severe	3-15 km	Vulcanian	yearly	Ruiz, 1985
4	cataclysmic	10-25 km	Vulc/Plinian	10s of years	Galunggung, 1982
5	paroxysmal	>25 km	Plinian	100s of years	Mt. St. Helens, 1980
6	colossal	>25 km	Plin/Ultra-Plinian	100s of years	Krakatau, 1883
7	super-colossal	>25 km	Ultra-Plinian	1000s of years	Tambora, 1815
8	mega-colossal	>25 km	Ultra-Plinian	10,000s of years	Yellowstone, 2.2 million years ago

Where's the Action?

Active Volcanoes by Region

- **80** Africa
- **6** Antarctica
- **1** Arctic Ocean
- **38** Australia
- **34** Europe/West Asia
- **139** North America/Central America
- **118** North Asia/Japan
- **65** South America
- **99** South East Asia

Volcanoes in the U.S.

State	Number
Alaska	108
Arizona	9
California	24
Colorado	1
Idaho	6
Hawaii	19
Nevada	7
New Mexico	16
Oregon	16
Utah	6
Washington	9
Wyoming	2

Some Active Volcanoes in the U.S.

Name	Last Eruption
Shasta, CA	1786
Rainier, WA	1894
Wrangell, AK	1902
Novarupta, AK	1912
Mt. St. Helens, WA	1986
Mauna Loa, HI	1984
Makushin, AK	1987
Kiska, AK	1990
Long Valley, CA	1996
Okmuk, AK	1997
Kilauea, HI	presently

A Lot on Our Plates

MAP KEY

Borders of Tectonic Plates

△ Pacific Ring of Fire

▲ Other Volcanic Activity

Volcanoes occur. But why?

We live on a crust of rock that floats like a raft on the sea of fluid magma. Make that, floats like rafts, plural. Earth's crust isn't one piece. It's cracked into a dozen or more pieces called *tectonic plates*, which are outlined on the map. Some plates contain both continent and ocean.

Because the fluid mantle underneath is moving, so are the plates. And when they move, they either bump into each other, pull away from each other, or scrape past each other. Volcanoes usually occur at the places where two plates meet and magma under pressure can be squeezed to the surface.

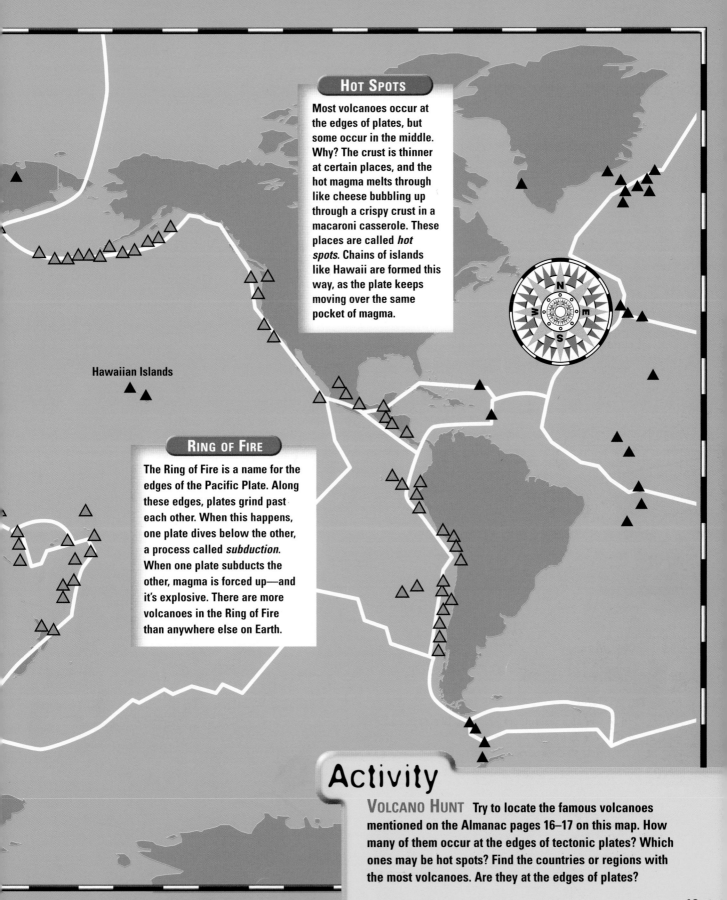

HOT SPOTS

Most volcanoes occur at the edges of plates, but some occur in the middle. Why? The crust is thinner at certain places, and the hot magma melts through like cheese bubbling up through a crispy crust in a macaroni casserole. These places are called *hot spots*. Chains of islands like Hawaii are formed this way, as the plate keeps moving over the same pocket of magma.

Hawaiian Islands

RING OF FIRE

The Ring of Fire is a name for the edges of the Pacific Plate. Along these edges, plates grind past each other. When this happens, one plate dives below the other, a process called *subduction*. When one plate subducts the other, magma is forced up—and it's explosive. There are more volcanoes in the Ring of Fire than anywhere else on Earth.

Activity

VOLCANO HUNT Try to locate the famous volcanoes mentioned on the Almanac pages 16–17 on this map. How many of them occur at the edges of tectonic plates? Which ones may be hot spots? Find the countries or regions with the most volcanoes. Are they at the edges of plates?

DEEP SECRETS

You find yourself in a strange place underwater. Suddenly, the ground splits apart and oozes lava, heating up the water to a cozy 572° F (300° C), about as hot as a blow torch. The lava hardens into fluffy-looking pads.

Chimneys 35 feet (11 m) tall sprout up and belch boiling hot chemicals. Clouds of sulfur-eating bacteria swarm and feast on the minerals. Giant tubeworms stretch twice the length of a basketball player and sway in the heat, combing the murky water for food. Clams the size of a small car camp nearby waiting for a meal.

This place really exists, but it is so far under the surface of the water that no human being can go there without very special protection. The pressure of the water thousands of feet below the surface would crush a diver, even if the water were cooler. These deepest sea environments, known as hydrothermal vents, were discovered in 1977. First we had to invent special machines called submersibles. They can take the hazardous temperature, the crushing pressure, the complete darkness, and the corrosive chemicals in the water. They can send back pictures so scientists can learn about this wild and bizarre place.

We know from the pictures that the ocean floor is always changing, and volcanic activity is the reason. When tectonic plates pull apart under the sea, cracks form. Hot magma flows up and fills in the cracks. The cracks form more easily in the ocean than on land, because Earth's crust under the ocean is only 3 to 5 miles (5 to 8 km) thick, as compared to 20 to 25 miles (32 to 40 km) thick under land. New magma means hot water, new rocks in new strips of ocean floor, new chemicals in the water. All this newness is a perfect breeding ground for mysterious life-forms.

tubeworms

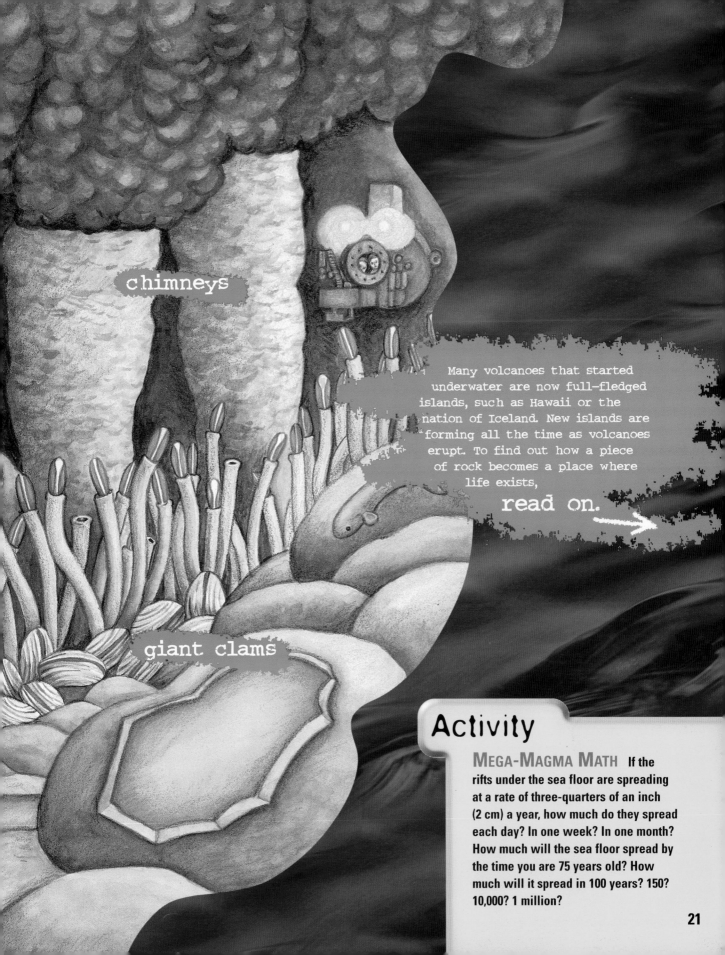

chimneys

Many volcanoes that started underwater are now full-fledged islands, such as Hawaii or the nation of Iceland. New islands are forming all the time as volcanoes erupt. To find out how a piece of rock becomes a place where life exists,

read on.

giant clams

Activity

MEGA-MAGMA MATH If the rifts under the sea floor are spreading at a rate of three-quarters of an inch (2 cm) a year, how much do they spread each day? In one week? In one month? How much will the sea floor spread by the time you are 75 years old? How much will it spread in 100 years? 150? 10,000? 1 million?

How to Build an Island
in Ten Easy Steps

1
IT CAME FROM THE SEA
November 14, 1963

Off the coast of Iceland, two tectonic plates wrench away from each other. As they pull apart, the seam between them spreads open and molten magma erupts from below to fill in the gap. The lava piles up, forming a cone.

2
BIRTH OF AN ISLAND
November 17, 1963

A volcanic cone pops above water level. An island is born: Surtsey. An island, yes—but this island is just lifeless, steaming rock.

3
FLY-BY
November to December 1963

In nearby Iceland, snow buntings, fulmars, and geese happily munch on berries and seeds. The growing chill in the air causes them to migrate over the water, seeking warmer regions. They happen to fly over the new rock in the neighborhood.

4
UNPACKING
November to December 1963

As the birds wheel overhead, nature calls, and they leave little bundles called droppings. These droppings are full of bacteria, fungus, and undigested seeds. Some birds touch down, depositing seeds stuck to their feet on the rock. The seeds are dormant.

5
THERE'S A FUNGUS AMONG US
January to November 1964

The droppings build up, and the bacteria and fungus begin to break the rock down into soil fertile and rich in mineral content. Dust is also blown onto the bare rock, adding to the thin soil layer. Wind and rain also do their part to wear the rock down into soil.

Surtsey Island at age twenty, after plant and animal life was established.

What else can happen when a volcano interacts with the ocean? Turn to the next page —and Wave Good-bye.

6 RETURN TRIP

November 1964

Birds again migrate over the island and make more deposits. This time seeds strike pay dirt.

7 READY, SET, SPROUT!

June 3, 1965

Scientists find Surtsey's first plant: a slip of sea rocket, growing out of the rough black pebbly beach. Would there be more?

8 PLANTS A-PLENTY

1967 to 1968

Yes! Other plants called sea sandwort and lyme grass begin to take hold. They form mats in the sand, helping to form sand dunes. Ducks arrive, joining the gulls and plovers already nesting there.

9 CALLING ALL BIRDS

1968

All the plant life brings the attention of more birds, which leave more droppings. The droppings appeal to insects and bacteria, which start to eat and multiply. More than sixty species of birds stop by Surtsey on their migratory route. Some begin to make nests. Butterflies are blown over by the sea winds.

10 ALIVE

1970

Birds peep from nests in the crags on Surtsey's lava cliffs, now as tall as a seven-story building. Small bushes and trees take root. Seals crawl up on the shore to bask in the Sun. A baby ecosystem has been formed.

Activity

BUILD IT YOURSELF Start with a sterile island, such as Krakatau after the 1883 explosion. Which birds, plants, and so forth would you import to start life on your island? Think about the food chain, including plants, animals, and conditions. Now grow an island from the bottom up! Note: There are videos and research available on the return of life to Mount St. Helens you can use for background.

Wave Good-

Rakata, Indonesia, August 27, 1833

Four gigantic explosions rock the 4.3 mile (7 km) island, which sits at a place where the Indo-Australian plate subducts the Pacific plate. The volcano Krakatau is blowing up—and telling the whole world about it. The third of these eruptions is the single most violent explosion on Earth in our time, its awesome power reinforced by the steam produced when seawater rushes into the collapsed cone. The noise can be heard 2,200 miles (3,540 km) away in Australia.

This Plinian/Ultra-Plinian eruption, equal to 200 million tons (181 million tonnes) of TNT, blasts out a pile of rock equal to half the island. A pillar of smoke and ash three times as high as Mt. Everest rises into the atmosphere. Its dust cloud will turn day into night in the surrounding areas and later spend a year circling Earth, causing red sunsets.

The energy of the blast makes the sea floor twitch. Small waves begin to form, building as they rush away in all directions. By the time the largest wave reaches Java and Sumatra, it is a terrifying wall of water as high as a twelve-story building.

In the harbors, the wave sinks more than five thousand boats. A ship is carried to a forest a couple of miles inland and dumped into the treetops. Now 36,000 people are dead and 160 villages are ruined. The wave keeps going.

Moving as fast as a jet airplane, it tears through the Indian Ocean around the Cape of Good Hope and into the Atlantic Ocean. A day and a half after the eruption, people comment on the high tides in the English Channel, on the other side of the world.

SUMATRA

Rakata

Krakatau

JAVA

INDIAN OCEAN

—bye

A Ripple in the Ocean, A Killer on the Shore

Tsunami is the Japanese word for a monster wave that reaches shore. But if you were flying above one, you wouldn't even see it. That's because these waves go down thousands of feet in the ocean and cover such a huge distance. There are hundreds of miles between crests, and the crests themselves may be just a few feet tall. But there is so much force behind the waves—called momentum—that they can travel great distances without losing much energy.

Near the shore, the approaching waves begin to interact with the shallower ocean floor. They slow down, but they pile up on each other and pull back. All the water is sucked away from shore. Harbors empty. Fish flop on the sand. Curious people come to take a look at what's going on—and can get killed by their curiosity. Why? The withdrawing of the sea is always followed by the tsunami's shattering collapse on shore.

AUSTRALIA

Activity

SAVE THE DAY Say that a tsunami the size and speed of the one you've just read about was generated by a volcanic eruption off the coast of Peru. Using a map, figure out which land masses would be in danger. Then figure out how long it would take for the tsunami to reach them. How many people live in these places, especially in coastal cities? Use an atlas to help make an evacuation plan that could save the day.

If It Sounds Like

Kilauea, Hawaii, 1872

The noise made by the bubbling lava is not great, heard as we heard it from our lofty perch. It makes three distinct sounds— a rushing, a hissing, and a coughing or puffing sound; and if you stand on the brink and close your eyes it is no trick at all to imagine that you are sweeping down a river on a large low-pressure steamer, and that you hear the hissing of the steam about her boilers, the puffing from her escape pipes, and the churning rush of water abaft [behind] her wheels.

"The Great Volcano of Kilauea," Mark Twain

Mark Twain

Vent, Kilauea Crater Floor, Hawaii

a Volcano...

Mark Twain wrote about the noises at Kilauea more than one hundred years ago, and today, people are still listening to volcanoes. And what they hear could save lives.

Scientist Milton Garces spent a week on the slope of the Arenal volcano in the rain forest of Costa Rica, listening to explosions, hissing, and chugging sounds like those of a train. He wondered if he could use those sounds to find out what was happening inside the volcano—maybe even to help predict volcanic eruptions.

Perfect Pitch

Garces had become interested in volcanoes while he was studying the effects of sound under the ocean. He learned that underwater volcano hunters needed to be able to tell the noise of erupting volcanoes apart from background ocean noise. But he figured it would be easier to study volcanoes on land. He soon found that volcanoes produce a wide variety of sounds. They range from low-pitched rumbles that humans can't hear but can feel, like the passing of a jet plane, all the way up to high-pitched whines and whooshes.

The rumbles are called infrasound ("below sound"), and Garces found out that they are a volcano's most revealing noise. Some infrasound comes from exploding bubbles of gas and rock that propel magma and other particles into the air. Infrasound also comes from magma flow deep inside Earth.

Trapped in a Bubble

Exactly what makes the rumbles? Scientists think gas bubbles in streams of magma expand and contract as pressure changes. The growls they make are trapped in the magma that rises through passages that lead to the vent of a volcano. The surface of the magma acts like the head of a drum, and the sound vibrations travel through the air.

Milton Garces and his colleague Michael Buckingham have collected an amazing amount of information that has helped them make models of the infrasound "fingerprint" of volcanoes. They now are sure that the amount of gas dissolved in magma determines how violent an eruption will be. And models that translate the sounds coming from a volcano into information almost as they happen are available now and continue to be improved.

A volcano can have such far-reaching effects, so that's good news for all of us. But for the five hundred million people living close to a volcano, it may be the difference between life and death.

Activity

LISTEN HERE Listening can lead to greater understanding of a scientific or mechanical process. For this activity, choose a familiar machine around the house, such as the toilet, the washing machine, or the refrigerator. Spend some time with it—a complete cycle for the washing machine, half an hour with the refrigerator. Sit so you can't see the machine, either wearing a watch or with a clock in sight. Keep a log of the sounds you hear: clicks, whirrs, whooshes, etc. Describe them as thoroughly as possible, and note the time each sound starts, changes pitch, volume, or quality, and ends. Using your log and your knowledge of what the machine does, try to figure out exactly what part of the process each noise signifies.

Courage Under Fire

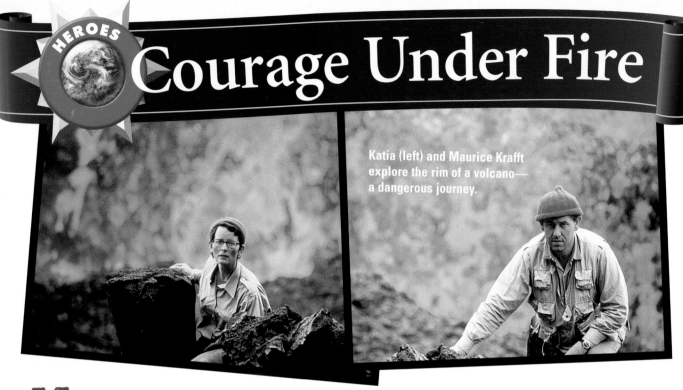

Katia (left) and Maurice Krafft explore the rim of a volcano— a dangerous journey.

Maurice and Katia Krafft spent more than twenty years racing to the scene of exploding volcanoes. Their tools were cameras, maps and rock hammers; the Kraffts were filmmakers and photographers as well as scientists. Their films and pictures are unforgettable, showing volcanoes up so close you can almost feel the heat and smell the sulfur.

The Kraffts wanted to show the dangers of eruptions so vividly that people would know what to expect and could be prepared. They knew such knowledge could save lives. Take Ruiz, an active volcano in Colombia that erupted in 1985. A mud slide triggered by the volcano's melted ice cap roared through a river valley, killing more than twenty-three thousand people. They all could have been saved simply by moving to higher ground, but local authorities didn't take scientists' warnings seriously.

To get the most powerful images, the Kraffts often put themselves at risk. They scampered along crumbling lava shelves hot enough to melt their shoes. They rowed a boat around a lake full of sulfuric acid concentrated enough to dissolve a human. They were lucky that time—they only lost the top layers of flesh off their fingers.

But Maurice and Katia's luck ran out one day in June 1991. While in Japan filming the eruption of Mt. Unzen, they got caught in a poisonous, glowing cloud of hot ash and gas. Along with thirty-five other people on the volcano, they perished. But they left behind a priceless legacy for volcanology: 2 million feet (609,600 m) of film, 20 tons (18 tonnes) of volcanic artifacts, hundreds of thousands of photographs. And now others are pursuing their goals of serving science and saving lives.

Steve and Donna O'Meara of Volcano, Hawaii, are not professional volcanologists. But they are experts in the field. They've visited seventy eruptions, photographing, observing, and, most of all, trying to help people in harm's way and make them aware of the seriousness of their situation. In Arenal, Costa Rica, the O'Mearas were appalled to find a local hotel giving out maps to the site of the eruption, even while boulder-sized lava blocks rolled down the slopes. "On the road up

Steve and Donna O'Meara have made volcanoes their life.

the mountain, we passed a father and a child, trying to read the map," Steve recalls. "Luckily, I got them to turn back."

It's not easy to make people turn back. Many whose homes are near volcanoes farm for a living, because volcanic soil is fertile. Leaving their homes for very long could mean starvation. But with world populations growing, more and more people will be living on the edge of disaster. Areas around certain volcanoes, such as Mount Vesuvius in Italy, are crowded with houses. Learning to predict eruptions more accurately is critical.

Just a few miles from the O'Mearas' home, at Kilauea, research on volcano prediction has been going on for some time. Scientists at the Hawaiian Volcano Observatory there are studying Kilauea, the most active volcano on the planet, to help perfect a system that will tell them if the ground beneath the volcano is swelling with magma—an early sign that an eruption is going to happen. The system uses receivers connected to the satellite Global Positioning System.

The system may be operational soon. Meanwhile, Steve and Donna O'Meara cherish the beauty and excitement of living near Kilauea. "There's always something happening," says Donna. "Steam is hissing out, and there are earthquakes almost every day—two-hundred-foot lava fountains are common. Sometimes we hold our breath, but we feel alive in their presence."

Are Volcanoes in Your Future?

Do you think you may want to be a volcanologist? Besides having a strong fascination and curiosity about volcanoes and how they work, you'll need to have a college degree in geology, mathematics, biology, or a related field, and maybe even a Ph.D. in geology. What can you do now? Junior high and high school science and math classes, as well as computer and writing classes, will help prepare you to do field work, write research papers, and collect data.

After all that hard work, the job can be rewarding. You'll be able to help reduce the risk to people living near volcanoes. You'll spend a lot of time outdoors and may travel to faraway places, like Chile or Russia. Plus, for people interested in how Earth works, volcanology can be exciting and fast paced. "It's a branch of geology where things actually happen quickly," says Scott Rowland, a volcanologist who works with the University of Hawaii. "Watching a volcano erupt is much more exciting than watching a beach erode or a glacier move."

Steam rises as lava pours into the ocean at Kilauea, Hawaii.

VOLCANO Lite

Volcanoes can be catastrophic events, but everything has its light side. With volcanoes, even the light side can be truly amazing.

India, 1883 A young woman goes outside, shields her eyes, and sees— a green Sun. She is mystified, but she would be even more surprised to learn that a faraway volcano caused it. In Trinidad at the same time, a woman looks up and is alarmed to see the Sun is BLUE! What is going on?

Ash from the explosive eruption of Krakatau has circulated in the stratosphere, scattering the Sun's rays and making the Sun appear different colors in different places. (You remember that sunlight has all the colors in the rainbow?)

Mount Erebus, Antarctica
There's gold in that volcano! Miners found gold condensed from volcanic gases on Mt. Erebus. Other elements that can be present in volcanoes include silver and copper.

Volcano Scramble
Unscramble these five unforgettable volcanoes

1. tonum vviuuess
2. alakiue
3. nmotu eelp
4. omtun buntapio
5. kkaaatru

Answers to Scramble: 1. Mount Vesuvius 2. Kilauea 3. Mount Pele 4. Mount Pinatubo 5. Krakatau

HAWAII, THEN AND NOW

In Hawaii, people still make offerings to the goddess Pele. While they see her as gentle, loving, and able to create new land, they also know she can be jealous and unpredictable, with a "volcanic" personality. The story goes that when her temper flares, she chucks fiery lava at anyone who makes her angry. To this day, people still throw flowers and gifts into volcanoes to please her.

The Solar System, Then and Now
Volcanoes can happen on other planets, too. Mount Olympus on Mars is a volcano three times as big as Mt. Everest. Io, a moon of Jupiter, has so many volcanoes on it that the whole surface is flowing with lava. It looks like a cheese pizza.

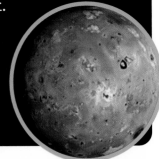

Tongue Twisters

These are all names of active volcanoes.
How many can you say correctly?

1 Popocatepetl, Mexico
2 Bezymianny, Kamchatka
3 Shishaldin, Alaska
4 Kliuchevskoi, Russia
5 Ixtaccihuatl, Mexico
6 Tongariro, New Zealand
7 Ruapehu, New Zealand
8 Niaragongo, Zaire
9 Niamuragira, Zaire
10 Hualala, Hawaii

Answers to Tongue Twisters:
1. Poe-poe-cah-TEH-petal
2. Beh-zee-mee-AN-ee
3. Shee-SHAWL-din
4. Klee-you-CHEV-skoy
5. Icks-tock-see-WAT-al
6. Tong-ah-REE-row
7. Rue-ah-PAY-who
8. Nee-ah-rah-GONG-go
9. Nee-ah-moo-rah-GEE-rah
10. Who-ah-LAH-lah

MAGMA Mirth

What did the volcano say to the mountain?
I lava you!

What did the volcano father do when his kids stole his lava?
He erupted!

How do you know if a mountain is a volcano?
Just ash it.

What do volcanoes eat their dinner on?
Tectonic plates.

What does baby lava call its parents?
Mag-Ma and Mag-Pa.

What do you call the Volcano Bill of Rights?
The Magma Carta.

What did the ice-cream server ask the volcano?
Do you want that in a cone?

What kind of volcano does a trout fear most?
A fissure (FISH-yer) volcano.

What happened when the volcano put on a play?
It was a bomb.

Uruapan, Mexico, 1943

Dominic Pulido, a farmer, gets ready to plant his cornfield. Wait a minute! Something is already growing there. Here are his own words.

"In the afternoon I joined my wife and son, who were watching the sheep, and inquired if anything new had occurred, since for two weeks we had felt strong tremors in the region. Paula replied that she had heard noise and thunder underground. Scarcely had she finished speaking when I, myself, heard a noise, like thunder during a rainstorm, but I could not explain it, for the sky above was clear and the day was peaceful, as it is in February.

"At 4 P.M., I left my wife to set fire to a pile of branches when I noticed that a grotto [grove] which was situated on one of the knolls of my farm, had opened . . . and I saw that it was a kind of fissure that had a depth of only half a meter. I set about to ignite the branches again, when I felt a thunder, the trees trembled, and I turned to speak to Paula; and it was then I saw how, in the hole, the ground swelled out and raised itself two or two and one-half meters high, and a kind of smoke or fine dust—gray, like ashes— began to rise up in a portion of the crack. Immediately more smoke began to rise, with a hiss or whistle, loud and continuous, and there was a smell of sulfur. I then became greatly frightened."

Dominic Pulido and his wife had witnessed the birth of a volcano, Paricutín. By eight the next morning, the "baby" was 32 feet (10 m) high. Most of the explosive activity was in the first year, when the cone grew to 1,100 feet (335 m). By the time it went dormant, in 1952, it was 1,390 feet (424 m) tall.

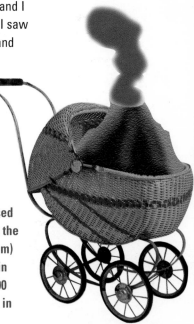

Final Project:
To Blast, or Not to Blast

Pretend you have to solve the problem of global warming. You know that a volcano has the power to cool temperatures worldwide. You know how volcanic particles in the upper atmosphere can cause temperatures to drop. So how about blowing up a volcano on purpose to deliberately cause the hot spell to break?

ANSWERS
Solve-It-Yourself Mystery, page 14:
A volcano began erupting at least eight months ago, probably more, when the calendar was last turned. From the condition of the buildings and the type of slope and lava, you can tell that the volcano erupted basaltic (pahoehoe) lava. That means it wasn't a violent explosion. Also, there are no signs of flames or debris. But the eruption must have lasted long enough to release plenty of gas. In fact, gas is still leaking out. Either sulfur dioxide or carbon dioxide suffocated the bird as it flew over the crater. And you can still smell hydrogen sulfide (rotten eggs) in the air.

The town center and the farm were west of the volcano—away from the direction the fumes and any ash would have been blown by prevailing winds. Hydrogen sulfide mixed with raindrops became acid rain. You figure that acid rain polluted the streams and ponds and eventually killed the crops, both as raindrops falling from the sky and in the buckets of pond water used for irrigation. The cow was killed by eating grass contaminated with the white fluoride dust you noticed.

With nothing to eat, most villagers left—probably by boat, leaving the harbor empty. The two you found might have been too frail to go with them, but luckily had enough emergency supplies to survive. What caused the worldwide cooling that sent you to explore in the first place? You reason that an explosion lasting so many months could release enough sulfuric acid and ash into the atmosphere to make a haze that blocked out the Sun's rays.

Gather friends or teammates around and:

1. Debate the pros and cons. Is it ethical to cause this kind of change? How much should we try to affect the weather?

2. What would be the worldwide consequences?

3. Study maps to pick the right volcano. It should be dormant at the moment.

4. Study population centers. You want to pick one that affects the fewest people.

5. Study weather patterns. You have to know what the prevailing winds are.

6. Study plate tectonics. Will your actions set off shock waves that will jar other volcanoes into action? How about tsunamis?

7. Make an evacuation plan for those people nearby.

8. Try to figure out how big an explosion you need. Use examples in this book such as Tambora and Krakatau to see how big a blast you need to achieve your objective.